DERB
Ghost

Prepare to be frightened by these terrifying tales
from around Derbyshire

By

Jill Armitage

BRADWELL
BOOKS

Published by Bradwell Books
9 Orgreave Close Sheffield S13 9NP
Email: books@bradwellbooks.co.uk

British Library Cataloguing in Publication Data: a catalogue
record for this book is available from the British Library.

1st Edition
ISBN: 9781902674629

Print: Gomer Press, Llandysul, Ceredigion SA44 4JL
Design by: jenksdesign@yahoo.co.uk

CONTENTS

INTRODUCTION

Derbyshire is in the dead centre of England with a fifteen-mile stretch of the M1 motorway threading its way from north to south. Looking down on the speeding traffic are the great Hardwick Hall, the ruins of Sutton Scarsdale Hall and the impressive Bolsover Castle, just three of the many haunted country houses dotted across Derbyshire's spectral landscape. Spirits that occupy stately piles give us a taste of social history, but because ghosts can appear just about anywhere, other supernatural entities remain tantalisingly anonymous. With so much paranormal activity to choose from, our task has been to select haunted places that are easily accessible and hauntings that are varied as well as spine-chilling.

The number of paranormal books I have written is well into double figures, so it's not surprising that people often ask me, 'Have you seen a ghost?' The answer has to be 'yes and no'! It's very rare for people to actually see a ghost; maybe a shadow caught in peripheral vision, but a full-blown manifestation tends to be the exception rather than the rule. I've sensed them, smelt them, felt them and heard them. With the advent of digital cameras, like many other people I've seen an amazing number of spirit manifestations in the form of orbs on my photographs. It's been theorised that orbs are spirit energy not normally visible to the human eye, which can be captured by increasingly sensitive cameras. In the pages that follow you will find a collection of stories from fifty of Derbyshire's most haunted places.

Some of the stories are well known and have probably been embellished with the number of tellings, while others, which appear here for the first time in print, are my own experiences and those of honest, reliable and publicity-shy individuals. Some have occurred very recently and are still happening, so I hope you enjoy the book and take the opportunity to visit some of the sites – and if you encounter any form of apparition, do let us know.

Jill Armitage

THE HAUNTED HOUSES OF
NORTH DERBYSHIRE

Hardwick Hall and **Hardwick Old Hall** are undoubtedly two of the most visited stately homes in the country. From their combined perch on a limestone ridge they dominate the surrounding area – magnificent statements of the wealth and authority of their builder, the indomitable Bess of Hardwick, Countess of Shrewsbury. She was undoubtedly the greatest of all the Elizabethan dynasts – the stuff of legends; charismatic, forceful yet romantic; the great matriarch who started the Devonshire dynasty.

Bess was born at Hardwick in 1521 and married four times. Only a year after her final marriage to George Talbot, the sixth Earl of Shrewsbury, they became custodians to Mary, Queen of Scots, who was to be kept under house arrest and moved around their other palatial homes. This put an enormous strain on the marriage and in 1583 they separated. Bess returned to her birthplace and childhood home at Hardwick, which on June 2nd 1583 she bought outright for £9,500 from her brother James's estate. He had died bankrupt in London's Fleet Prison in 1581. She set about embellishing her rural retreat to suit her needs, but when the Earl died in 1590 their vast fortune became solely hers. Shrewd investment had made her one of the richest women in the land and she began work on a new hall a few yards from the old one.

The Magnificent Hardwick Hall – more glass than wall.
[Reproduced with the kind permission of the National Trust]

On October 4th 1597 Elizabeth Hardwick, Dowager Countess of Shrewsbury, moved into her new residence and resided there for ten years until her death in 1608 aged 87, but her spirit still haunts Hardwick Hall. In the stately rooms of the south wing, where Bess had her own private apartments, a previous long-term housekeeper named Mrs Frances Stent was woken in her bedroom by the figure of Bess standing over her. *'She spoke kindly to me, and thanked me for looking after her house and its contents so beautifully,'* said Mrs Stent. For a 20th-century housekeeper to receive such a gracious vote of thanks from the lips of a 17th-century mistress of the house must surely have been an impressive and unique experience.

In the empty corridor approaching this apartment, a Yorkshire Terrier owned by a subsequent housekeeper often barked and whined excitedly. Animals are very sensitive to spirits, so could this little dog have been aware of some presence which is usually invisible to humans?

A presence is often felt in the doorway of the chapel, and staff have frequently reported seeing a lady dressed in blue wandering around the building, oblivious to the fact that people were watching her. Phantom aromas have been reported in the High Chamber, where the fragrance of citrus and other exotic fruits sometimes predominate. A ghost cat is said to favour the needlework room and the chapel landing, but, according to one lady custodian, the Blue Bedroom is the centre of all the hauntings. Visitors to this room frequently report the feeling of being watched, while others claim to have been touched or spoken to by an invisible personality. Many people say there is a presence within the room, which is icy cold, and the bed is frequently found to have an indentation as if some unseen individual has been lying there. One visitor reported seeing a woman dressed in grey standing by the fireplace. The figure walked across the room, straight through the rope barrier that marked the public route, and disappeared as she reached the bed.

The ruined Hardwick Old Hall is Bess's remodelled family home, now in the care of English Heritage. On one occasion Nicola, the custodian of Hardwick Old Hall, had just arrived at work and was walking down the path towards the hall when she got the feeling that someone was behind her. She turned, intending to tell the person that the hall wasn't yet open, but stopped in disbelief. Standing just behind her was a figure which she described as looking like vertical heat waves. It wasn't a hot day and there was no explanation for this strange phenomenon which, after a few seconds, simply disappeared.

Christine is another member of staff who has seen the same thing, which she described as wavy lines outlining one side of a small figure, but this time it was inside the West Lodge of Hardwick Old Hall. According to staff and visitors there is one particular room here that has a strange atmosphere that makes people feel uncomfortable. Dogs don't like it either. They have been known to go to the far corner of the room and bark at something only they can see or sense.

The West Lodge ghost likes playing practical jokes on new members of staff who are working alone for the first time at the Old Hall. That's when things start to happen. One of the doors repeatedly closes on its own, books fall to the floor, footsteps are heard running in the empty upstairs rooms and some staff members have seen that faint image like the wavy outline of a small person.

The brooding ruins of Hardwick Old Hall sit next to the New Hall

After spending the day helping out at Bolsover Castle, Nicola called in at Hardwick Old Hall to catch up on some paperwork. It was early evening and the place was deserted as she let herself in through the main door. She then went to unlock the glass-fronted door leading into the shop, but the handle came away in her hand. Her first thought was that someone had been trying to break in or alternatively that someone was playing a prank on her. In order to fix the door she searched for the screws, but as they were missing, she removed two from the other side of the door to secure it overnight. She left at about 9 pm, but next morning when she arrived at work these screws had also been removed and were missing. She was the only person in the building and all the other doors were locked. Because at some point in the past West Lodge was used as a schoolroom, staff now put any strange experiences down to mischievous, ghostly children playing tricks.

The grounds of Hardwick Hall used to be the haunt of a monk described as having a luminous face. He's been seen by people driving through the park, National Trust employees, several estate workers and two police officers. In fact his appearances have been so numerous they were often reported in the *Derbyshire Times*.

One autumn day, a man and his dog were walking along an avenue near Hardwick Hall. The day was still, and the ankle-deep drifts of decaying leaves lay unruffled by any breath of wind. Except for the sound of their own footsteps, all was silent. Suddenly the dog began to cringe with obvious fright, its coat bristled with fear and it recoiled as though from some invisible source of danger. The dog's mystified owner saw that the carpet

Barlborough Hall has indelible bloodstains on the floor and a bride who haunts the battlements

of leaves along the road was being silently stirred by invisible feet as the unseen pedestrian proceeded along his way.

Barlborough Hall Prep School is a 16th-century Grade I listed building just off junction 30 of the M1. The hall's history is tangled with religious persecution and it has retained many original features such as the spy holes of the priest hide, used to conceal Catholic priests. Sadly this wasn't always successful and the ghost of a recusant priest, murdered while in concealment, is said to haunt an upper floor. Despite many attempts to remove them, his bloodstains are alleged to have left indelible stains on the floor of the room.

The Grey Bride is said to walk the corridors after tragedy struck on her wedding day. As she left the hall to make her way to the nearby church, news was received that her groom had met with a fatal accident when his coach overturned on his way to the church. His bride-to-be was totally devastated. She rushed back to the hall and threw herself from the battlements. It is said that from then on, whenever the moon is full, the ghost of the girl in her wedding dress can be seen drifting around the battlements.

Not many buildings in Britain occupy such a splendid position as **Bolsover Castle**, perched on the brow of a limestone ridge above the valley of the River Rother. A great example of Jacobean Romantic Architecture, standing almost chateau-like, this little castle evokes thoughts of medieval fortresses and pageantry, so it's not surprising to find that a castle has stood here since the 12th century.

The castle passed through a variety of owners until it was sold to Sir Charles Cavendish, son of Bess of Hardwick, in 1613. His son William continued the work after his death, and given his reputation as a womaniser and great philanderer, much of the decoration and many of the paintings suggest that William Cavendish was intent upon putting the little castle into the category of a private pleasure house. Many art historians have described the wall paintings and pictures as risqué subject matter, presumably intended for the personal pleasure of William Cavendish and his close friends. One member of staff while conducting a guided tour joked about Sir William being a bit of a ladies' man when suddenly she felt a ghostly push. As she lurched forward, she sprained her ankle.

Bolsover's imposing castle

William's remarkable skill in handling and training horses became so renowned that he was nicknamed the Horsemanship Duke, and here at Bolsover he built a Riding House to demonstrate those skills. The Riding House also has a viewing gallery where in his old age William sat and watched his horses being put through their paces, but is he still there watching? I had a strong sense of unease as I walked towards the viewing area and looked past the dummy boards into the riding house. I didn't know at the time, but those dummy boards of Sir William and his lady have been known to move on their own, and ghostly footsteps have been heard walking along this floor. I took a photograph and when it was processed I realised why I'd felt uneasy. I had caught a series of orbs – or light anomalies as they are also called – the first manifestation of ghosts.

When the team from Living TV's Most Haunted visited Bolsover Castle, they too captured various light anomalies here, and after hours, when all the doors are locked, security guards have seen lights and heard the sounds of horses being put through their paces.

All around the castle, people have reported being spoken to, pushed, slapped, tickled, pinched or having their clothing tugged in a childish or familiar way. Late one night a member of staff was walking through the walled fountain garden when she heard footsteps behind her. There was no one there. Ghostly knights have been seen walking along the top of the wall that surrounds the fountain garden, and visitors and volunteers have seen the apparition of a little boy who will take the hand of a visiting child and try to lead him/her around or encourage them to play.

Visitors hear the sound of marching feet and trotting horses coming up the south drive and see soldiers in Civil War costumes marching up and down the terrace range.

The Little Castle or Keep is a four-storey miniature version of a medieval castle, 18 metres (60 feet) square with turrets at each corner. People report a feeling of uneasiness here, strange lights have been seen and workmen have heard the swish of gowns. Staff and visitors have experienced the scent of pipe-smoke and perfume and even heard a man and woman laughing and joking rather intimately. Electrical equipment malfunctions in this area and a smoky figure is seen. Staff believe it is the old housekeeper, and feel her presence so strongly they greet her when entering.

From the top floor, one hundred steps descend directly to the pre-1617 vaulted basement where people report the smell of oranges, cucumber and other foodstuffs including sugared almonds, roast pork and mutton. There are also strange noises and lots of slaps and pinches are administered in this area.

Bolsover is certainly very active with spiritual energies, but there's also a feeling of calm and friendship; except on certain days when the castle appears to be very inhospitable. At these times, visitors say they feel like unwanted intruders being pushed along by an invisible force. It appears that even ghosts have their off days!

Renishaw Hall has been the Derbyshire seat of the Sitwell family for over 350 years and its paranormal activity is so strong that the 'Duke's Landing' on the first floor has been dubbed 'Ghost Passage' by the family. There's a grey-haired woman, wearing a white cap, and something like a two-tone blue crinoline, but the most charming is Henry, the last of the Sacheverells, a sickly child who drowned aged thirteen in 1726. He has become known as the kissing ghost because he has a rather surprising penchant for nestling up to lady guests and giving them a kiss.

The kissing ghost at Renishaw.
Courtesy the late Sir Reresby Sitwell

Renishaw Hall
Courtesy the late Sir Reresby Sitwell

Sutton Scarsdale Hall today presents a sad, melancholy appearance. It lies close to junction 29 of the M1 motorway at Heath, and from that distance, when the light is right, it gives the impression of romantic splendour. Close to it's a different matter. The great mansion is now a crumbling ruin that houses a plethora of ghosts.

The ruined Sutton Scarsdale Hall is one of the most haunted buildings around

For centuries Sutton Scarsdale was the seat of the Leake family, The earls of Scarsdale, but in 1820 it was bought by Richard Arkwright, the son of the famous industrialist. In 1920 the hall was put up for sale but no one wanted to live in this fabulous mansion. A speculator bought the property and desecrated it, selling lead from the roof and ripping out much of the interior which was shipped to America.

The fine work of Italian craftsmen was left open to the elements, ceilings began to collapse and chimneypieces executed by Italian masters hung in mid-air. Once the hall had been allowed to fall into ruin, an aura of mystery soon descended on the place. People began to whisper of ghostly encounters amid the mouldering ruins, and locals reported seeing a grey-looking figure, white lights and fleeting shadows flash across the windowless voids.

The building was soon nothing more than a crumbling shell in a deplorable and dangerous state and was earmarked for demolition, but fate intervened when Sir Osbert Sitwell of Renishaw Hall agreed to purchase the building simply to save it. English Heritage eventually took over, cleaned up the site and preserved the building for future generations. While a team of English Heritage workmen were making the structure safe, the basement and cellars were used as a store and workshop, and one part was the only area that was heated. One cold wintry day two work colleagues were warming themselves by the cellar stove during their tea break when they heard footsteps crossing the stone floor above and descending the stone steps, followed by voices coming from just outside the door. They listened in surprise because the interior of the hall was cut off from public access, but as they pulled open the cellar door they found the stairs empty and no one in sight.

This once great mansion is now no more than a sad, melancholy shell, and when the wind whispers through the swaying trees there is a distinctly eerie atmosphere and the ruin looks every bit the forbidding, haunted building. It's a very atmospheric place even in daylight, but at night its takes on a markedly

1789 & 1791 room settings from Sutton Scarsdale hall, now in
The Philadelphia Museum of Art
Supplied courtesy of the Philadelphia Museum of Art

sinister and menacing appearance. It's not surprising that for years there have been numerous tales of hauntings.

One story that had amazing repercussions originated as a bet in the 1960s between a Nottingham professor and a resident of Hillstown. The professor promised to pay the man one pound if he would agree to remain fastened to a post in the churchyard past the witching hour of midnight. The man, already inebriated, readily agreed, but was soon troubled by his eerie surroundings and ran, screaming, from the churchyard. The terrified man claimed that he had seen a ghost with no legs and wearing a white hood, with slits for eyes, glide through the churchyard.

Understandably this story flew round the neighbourhood, probably gaining much in the telling, and local ghost hunters flocked to the churchyard in the hope of seeing the 'white lady'.

There was so much interest that the local papers carried the story and in an article that appeared in the *Star* newspaper on June 29th 1967, a reporter interviewed the rector of St Mary's Church. He suggested that the ghost was probably one of the large white owls that glide between the bushes and trees, and circle the hall at night. Despite this possible explanation, attention still focused strongly on the probability that Sutton Scarsdale Hall and its adjoining churchyard were haunted.

Dog walkers noticed how their canine companions reacted strangely and it became a popular venue for local ghost-hunting groups. One group reported that a spirit threw stones at them. Others have reported lights of a mixed hue that appear and hover for a few seconds before vanishing. Footsteps are reportedly heard wandering around the building on floors and stairs that no longer exist and there's the phantom smell of tobacco in various parts of the structure.

The Chesterfield Psychic Research Society has visited the hall and church during daylight and at night, and on one occasion they saw a grey-looking figure appear and walk towards the back of the church. It made no sound as it disappeared round the corner of the building, unlike the noise of rustling leaves and snapping twigs under the feet of the would-be ghost hunters as they hurried after it. They found nothing, yet all had the unnerving feeling that a presence was watching them from the window voids of this once great house.

Tupton Hall was built in 1668 on the site of an earlier hall, and survives today, mainly in name, as a large comprehensive school. Our ghost story goes back to the time when the hall was the home of Mr Lord, a wealthy Chesterfield miller who was returning home one evening when he was waylaid and robbed by a masked highwayman. He was convinced that it was the family coachman, and, although the poor man swore his innocence, Mr Lord had him tried, convicted and hanged. Just before his execution, the man swore a curse on the family and predicted that disaster after disaster would follow.

So did his curse come true? The family died out and the hall was only saved from destruction because it was purchased in 1929 by the Derbyshire Education Committee, and opened as a grammar school in 1936. Then disaster struck when in 1938 the hall was badly burnt, totally destroying much of the magnificent Robert Adam interior. In August 1955, the then headmaster Mr

Tupton Hall has now been demolished but will the curse live on

Drabble hanged himself; a few days later the history teacher threw herself under a train; and the deputy headmaster dropped dead in October.

The school expanded greatly under the comprehensive system of the late 1960s but in 1974 another fire in the Art Block forecast the return of the jinx. In 1990, a great copper beech in the centre of the school came crashing down, demolishing one of the stairwells, and in 2000 it was announced that all the school buildings were in such a bad state they would need totally replacing. Perhaps the new build which will totally obliterate the old Tupton Hall will at last break the curse.

The Hall on Dronfield's High Street was built during the reign of Queen Anne in the 18th century. Its symmetrical facade is quite charming and possess a bygone elegance, but the house and garden are reputed to be haunted by a white lady. Several occupants have heard strange noises, and one owner believed a child had once been murdered there.

Dronfield Manor House is now the library

In 1967, the 18th-century **Manor House** at Dronfield was converted into the library and, despite a total revamp, it retains its period atmosphere and its ghosts. Ann is a cleaner there and told me that although she's never seen anything and doesn't mind the early-morning shifts, she always feels nervous in the building at night. Her colleague now refuses to work the evening cleaning shift, saying that she often felt as if she was being watched.

Situated just behind the Manor House is the Grade II listed Manor House Farm. Mr and Mrs Gwynn spent a year renovating the house, after which all manner of strange things began to happen. In the sitting room they heard a noise like someone running a stick over the fireplace and other inexplicable sounds. A decorator working alone in the sitting room heard someone go upstairs and use the toilet, yet there was no one else in the house.

Tapton House in the suburb of Chesterfield was the much-loved home of George Stephenson, the Railway King. His plans to run a railway from Leeds to Derby steamed straight through Chesterfield but encountered problems five miles south at Clay Cross. There it was necessary to dig a one-mile tunnel through Clay Cross hill and, in doing so, the navvies discovered iron and coal deposits. Stephenson, ever ready to seize a new idea, formed the Clay Cross Co to extract the rich minerals and in 1838 he leased Tapton House, where he lived until his death on August 12th 1848. He was laid to rest at Holy Trinity Church; but probably 'laid to rest' are inappropriate words considering the number of times he has been seen since in and around Tapton House.

George Stephenson statue outside Chesterfield Railway Station

In the 1920s the young daughter of a footman employed at Tapton House played regularly in the grounds, but on one occasion she and her friend ventured into the old coach house and climbed into a neglected coach to play. After a while, they became aware of an old gentleman standing in the corner watching them. He was of medium height, but appeared taller because of the tall 'stove-pipe' hat he was wearing. The girls left in a hurry and, fearing a reprimand, were reluctant to tell their parents. When they did eventually confess, the footman professed that he too had seen the ghost on many occasions. It was the great man himself, George Stephenson.

From 1931 to 1993 Tapton House was a school, and apparently there were many sightings during this time. On one occasion, a caretaker was sweeping a corridor on the first floor when she heard a masculine voice say quite clearly, 'You didn't bring my water up today!'

She looked up to see a total stranger. He was dressed in dated clothing, but he was quite normal in every other aspect. When he repeated the words, she made a mumbled apology and hurried off to find her husband. After telling him what had just happened, they returned to the now empty corridor. The only way the man could have left was through a locked door at the end of the corridor, but the door was still locked. Later, when shown a selection of photographs taken from portraits, without hesitation the caretaker selected the portrait of George Stephenson as the man she had seen.

Tapton House in Chesterfield

After a considerable revamp, in 1994 Tapton House was taken over by the Chesterfield College of Further and Higher Education, who are still there today, but the sightings have not stopped. Over the last few years there have been reports of doors mysteriously opening and closing, and masculine footsteps in the corridors. One former student told me that a portrait of George Stephenson that hangs in the hall has eyes that follow you around. Is this a vivid imagination or is George still keeping an eye on his old home?

Alfreton is an interesting town, within reach of some of Derbyshire's most attractive scenery. Part of the attractive 17th-century **Alfreton House** was used during the 1970s as a WRVS clothing depot. Members of the WRVS, while sorting and stacking clothing, often experienced phantom footsteps and strange vibrations, and no one would stay in the building alone. According to Mrs Joan Shacklock, the neatly piled baby clothes were regularly disturbed as if someone had sorted through them, despite it being impossible for anyone to gain access to do this. The door to the storeroom was kept locked, and there was never any sign of tampering, so could this be a pregnant ghost with a phantom pregnancy?

Alfreton House

The Hayes at Swanwick, two miles south of Alfreton, was a German prisoner of war camp between 1939 and 1945, and some of the prisoners dug a tunnel in a classic escape attempt. Five prisoners managed to crawl through the narrow passage and emerge into the nearby fields before the alarm was raised, but Oberleutnant Franz von Werra, posing as a Dutch airman, was actually seated in the cockpit of a plane at Hucknall Aerodrome in Nottinghamshire before he was arrested. This daring attempt and those that followed were made into a book and film in 1957 called *The One That Got Away*, but has his ghost actually returned?

The Garden House where German prisoners of war were held

After the war the Hayes was opened to the public for conferences, including the Writer's Summer School which I first attended in 2001. The wooden building that had housed the prisoners was then known as the Garden House and still had a rather austere atmosphere. The stairs were uncarpeted and small cell-like rooms branched off from the long central corridors. The escape tunnel from what had been re-numbered room 102 was still there, and apparently a cleaning lady working in that room had discovered tools under the floorboards.

No one was really too surprised when people started reporting inexplicable noises. A conference visitor was woken at 5.30 am by the unmistakable sound of heavy marching feet outside the Garden House, yet when she looked out of her window there was no one there. Another person heard the clatter of heavy boots on the wooden stairs early one morning, yet the stairs were carpeted. A woman attending a writers' conference apparently saw a man in German officer's uniform standing by her dressing table. Her room was number 102. The Garden House has since been demolished.

Carnfield Hall is a 15th-century hall situated on the B6019 road between Alfreton and South Normanton, built originally as the Manor House of South Normanton.

It has been described as the perfect haunted house with atmosphere. A shadowy figure has been seen at the bottom of the main staircase; strange noises like furniture being moved and footsteps are heard at dead of night; there are definite cold spots; and numerous visitors have sensed something unnatural about the hall. According to legend, every year Carnfield has a ghostly ball, a re-enactment of a party given to celebrate Robert

Revel's appointment as High Sheriff of Derbyshire in 1700. A team of ghost hunters investigating the hall made a recording in the Great Parlour and captured the sound of a harpsichord being played. Experts identified it as a rare organ harpsichord and, checking early inventories, it was found that such an instrument had been given as a wedding gift by the then owner, Sir Nicholas Wilmot, to his daughter in 1666. The hall has obviously known much music and laughter, and a TV crew filming at the hall captured shadowy hands, one with a great white lace cuff, raised as if in some dance movement.

According to local legend, a previous owner was murdered in his bed. Psychics, who knew nothing of this, claimed that someone was suffocated in what was his bedroom. His sad presence is felt more than seen, but there's a white lady who haunts the south-east bedroom and walks through a blocked-up door that would once have led to a dressing room and a maid's room. Surprisingly it is only women who see her, not men, and female guests have woken in the night to find her standing by the side of their bed, her pale face peering down at them.

The grounds are no less spiritually active. Three spirit children – two girls and a boy – are seen regularly playing bat and ball on one of the lawns. There's the ghost of a gamekeeper who walks in the park, and a ghostly carriage drawn by six horses makes its stately way along the old drive.

The Nightingale family first brought prosperity to the area of Lea and Holloway. Peter Nightingale (great-grandfather of Florence Nightingale, the Lady with the Lamp who brought nursing out of the dark ages)) had amassed a considerable fortune from lead mining, and in 1707 bought **Lea Hall** and became Lord of the Manor. Florence's parents built the nearby Lea Hurst, which is where, after the Crimean War, Florence Nightingale returned in August 1856 worn out and ill. From her bedside she continued to campaign for improvements in sanitation and public health and better conditions for British soldiers. Despite their moving away in later years, Lea Hurst remained in the Nightingale family until Louis Nightingale died in 1940. In 1951 it was presented to the Royal Surgical Aid Society and it became a home for the elderly. Residents and staff here have reported seeing the ghost of Florence wandering along a top corridor and down the stairs, and there are also reports of her restless spirit wandering round the grounds.

Lea Hurst, the former home of Florence Nightingale

The ruins of South Wingfield Manor

The 15th-century ruins of **South Wingfield Manor** stand on the ridge above the River Amber some two miles from Alfreton. The manor came to prominence when in 1569 its then owner the Earl of Shrewsbury and his wife Bess of Hardwick were made gaolers to Mary, Queen of Scots. For eighteen years she was moved around their palatial homes strung across Derbyshire.

Throughout her imprisonment Mary's Catholic supporters plotted to obtain her release and the final plot was named after a Derbyshire squire named Anthony Babington. Unfortunately, Queen Elizabeth's spymaster Francis Walsingham uncovered the plot and all involved, including Mary, Queen of Scots, were executed. Now her ghost is said to return to South Wingfield Manor. Surrounded by an azure light of indefinite shape, the ghostly figure of Mary has been seen gliding around the ruins and walking across the crypt, where she disappears through a blocked doorway. Several people have heard sounds similar to footsteps and a gardener has often smelt the scent of perfume around the entrance to the undercroft, even though alone and with no scented flowers in bloom.

Probably the most poignant ghosts encountered are those of Mary and Anthony Babington walking freely in the grounds, doing in death what would never have been allowed in their lifetimes. However, Mary and Anthony are not the only spirits that haunts the ruins of Wingfield Manor. A ghostly white cat is frequently seen wandering the house and gardens before slowly vanishing. Lights are seen in unoccupied areas and inexplicable sounds like moans, bangs, footsteps and whispering are heard coming from empty rooms.

South Wingfield Manor was almost demolished during the Civil War and is now in the care of English Heritage. Two workmen engaged in maintenance work had just finished and taken their tools and equipment back to their van when one of them realised he had left something behind. Returning alone to the crypt he encountered a full army of Parliamentary soldiers about to re-enact the destruction of the building.

The owners of **Goss Hall** on the slopes above Ashover can be traced back nine centuries; several are quite notable but the most distinguished and legendary is undoubtedly Sir Thomas Babington who purchased the manor around 1500. This prominent Derbyshire family were staunch Catholics and indisputably the most notorious member of the family was Sir Thomas's great, great grandson Anthony Babington who tried unsuccessfully to instate Mary Queen of Scots as Queen of England. There's a story that Anthony intended bringing Mary to Eddlestowe Hall, the family's other manor house in the area and allegedly there is a secret tunnel between there and Goss Hall that was to be used as an escape route. Local legend also maintains that Anthony Babington had to take refuge in the cellars of Goss Hall on at least one occasion when trying to escape. Sadly he was finally caught, tried and executed for high treason which meant that all his properties were forfeited to Queen Elizabeth. She passed Goss Hall to one of her favourites, Sir Walter Raleigh and our ghost story comes from the period when Goss Hall was in his possession.

Phantom fragrances or abstract odours as they are frequently called are often associated with spirit activity and it is not uncommon to detect abstract odours when dealing with the paranormal. These can be pleasant or pungent and people have smelt all manner of things, but when one occupant of Goss Hall insisted she could smell tobacco, the eminent Derbyshire writer Roy Christian brought up the Raleigh connection. Sir Walter Raleigh introduced tobacco to this country, so does his ghost still linger at Goss Hall. The smell was apparently so bad in the 1950s that it caused one owner to leave and the hall became almost a ruin, but after sympathetic restoration, it is now a very desirable private house.

The 1,000 acre **Overton Hall** estate on the hillside above Ashover originally belonged to the Overton family. It passed to the Hunts in 1327, the Hodgkinsons in 1599 then by marriage to the Banks family and so to Sir Joseph Banks, the distinguished naturalist. At the age of eighteen, Joseph Banks came into a considerable inheritance enabling him to pursue his keen interest in botany in adventurous style. In 1766 he undertook the first of his discovery voyages to Newfoundland, was made a Fellow of the Royal Society, then from 1768-71 accompanied Captain James Cook aboard HMS Endeavour acting as the supervisory scientist on the Royal Society's famed expedition to the South Seas. They returned with a vast collection of botanical specimens, and Sir Joseph planted a wide variety of rare trees and shrubs in the parklands and grounds of Overton Hall. It became known for its horticulture, but there were other things more sinister than plants buried there.

In 1884 when digging the foundations for a wall, seven skeletons (some say more) were unearthed. All were big, heavy men with their skulls broken. They were re-interred in Ashover churchyard but nothing was discovered to throw any light on the reason for the rather unorthodox burial in the grounds at Overton Hall. Some reports say they appeared to have been buried hastily, perhaps as a result of plague but that would not account for their damaged skulls.

Sir Joseph died on June 19th 1820 and the thirty roomed lumpish mansion passed to the Bright then the Jessop family. In the 1930's it was let to the Youth Hostel Association, then when war was declared in 1939, it was used initially by the boys of Derby Grammar School, then as an approved school followed by a residential home for the elderly.

With such a history it's not surprising to find that Overton Hall also has at least one ghost, so several years ago I was delighted to be invited to look round when it was being transformed into a private house. Despite the fact that in 1956, a story was reported in the press that the wife of a Pentecostal pastor living at Overton Hall had left because it was haunted, these new residents had not experienced anything. Then ironically, just two weeks ago, I was very fortunate to meet a lady who lives in part of Overton Hall which is now converted into several luxury homes. She and her husband have been there for almost six years and I was interested to know if they had experienced anything paranormal.

'Oh yes,' she said, 'although it took us a long time to realise it. A female figure would regularly pass our glazed back door and because the glass is frosted we just assumed it was our neighbour. Then one day after seeing the woman walk past, my husband arrived home and I asked if he'd just seen our neighbour. He shook his head. He hadn't seen anyone. I knew it was impossible for her to have disappeared without being seen, so we started to compare notes. We had both seen the mystery figure pass and because it had substance we each thought it was a neighbour.'

Now they realise that it's not. Over the years, the most regularly reported ghostly sighting at Overton Hall has been the figure of a woman seen walking across the forecourt. She is thought to be the third wife of one of the Jessops who resided there towards the end of the 19th century, and apparently she is still wandering around her former home.

Ogston Hall is well screened from the road as it stands on a prominence of high ground to the south of Ogston reservoir in the glorious Amber Valley. The hall has been built in four distinct stages and displays four very different styles of architecture, the oldest section being the West Wing dating back to Medieval Times. It is this wing that is said to be haunted by one of the last Revells – Leonard. In the 1880s, the West Wing was used as sleeping quarters for the female servants and around 1881 two maids were woken in the middle of the night by the sound of someone dragging a heavy object across the floor. Thinking it was an intruder, they alerted the male servants who slept across the courtyard.

A search was made in the house but no-one was discovered. The shouts of the hysterical females to the men servants could have disturbed the intruder yet this was discounted.

Many years later, Don Lees the Ogston estate gamekeeper stayed at the Hall while the family were away, and he not only heard the ghost, he also saw it. The story that circulated was that this unaccountable disturbance was the ghost of Leonard Revell, who had been hanged in 1723 for the murder of his servant in the West Wing of Ogston Hall. Is the ghostly sound, the re-enactment of this foul deed as Leonard Revell drags the corpse of his servant across the floor?

The registers of Shirland have an entry under 1723; April 29th. *Leonard Revell who was hanged for murder was buried at the backside of the chancel.*

With its gaunt, embattled façade frowning down from its 853ft high perch, for years **Riber Castle** was no more than a brooding ruin that dominated the skyline of Matlock and area. It has now undergone a revamp, but in the popular imagination, ruins and ghosts go hand in hand, so it acquired a reputation of being haunted. Although sightings are not regular, the most seen ghost is said to be a lady in blue who patrols the grounds and wonders through the empty corridors and rooms. One woman who saw her while walking her dogs described her as having untidy hair, a gentle expression and sad, shadowed eyes. Could this be Caroline Smedley the Wirksworth vicars daughter who, although given little recognition, took an active part in the formation and running of Smedley's Hydropathic Establishment, alongside her husband? Riber Castle was built by them as their family home.

At times people have also seen a figure in military uniform who not only marches round the walls, but through them too. He was witnessed by Mr & Mrs Linnett in 1973. Like many people who have had similar experiences, seeing him so fleetingly made them question whether he was there at all, or just a trick of the light?

CHURCHYARD HAUNTINGS

St Peter's Church is in the centre of **Derby.** It dates back to 1046 and served the most densely populated part of the town, so it's not surprising that in its churchyard there are more dead bodies than in any other graveyard in Derby. What makes this so bizarre is the fact that many were buried standing up to ease the overcrowding. In 1349, the Black Death killed one-third of the population of Derby, but one of the symptoms of the plague was a long, deep sleep or coma and many folks were buried prematurely. There are reports in St Peter's parish register of hands appearing out of the soil and trying to claw their way out of their shallow graves.

Spondon church and vicarage, now St Werburgh's House Nursing Home, has three ghosts: an old woman who sits in a rocking chair at an upstairs window gazing out forlornly at the rear garden, a monk and a fair-haired woman wearing a blue dress who walks through the grounds to the church. She was photographed in the church in the 1970s and the ghostly image is still considered to be a genuine exposure.

At St Peter's churchyard at **Chellaston**, a church grim has been seen. 'Grim' is a generic name for a spirit which associates with humanity and human dwellings. When a church was built or a churchyard consecrated, making a foundation sacrifice was one of a number of pagan practices which lasted into the early Christian era. It was believed that the first person to be buried in a graveyard returned in spirit to protect the dead from the ghosts and ghouls and other nefarious supernatural creatures that were believed to haunt such places. That's why, before any human was interred, a black dog would be sacrificed, thus creating a guardian spirit, known as the kirke-grim or church grim, and the church grim will never leave its designated graveyard. The Chellaston grim is described as being a huge, bear-like creature with a dirty, mangy coat. It seems to appear from thin air and walks silently in and around the graveyard, often pausing to survey its witnesses with large, saucer-like, glowing eyes before disappearing again.

The ghostly figure of a woman who haunts **Etwall** graveyard makes her appearances late at night. People who have walked past the graveyard have heard sobbing, but many believe this is not a ghost but the marble statue of a crying angel that comes alive at night and wanders round the graveyard looking at headstones.

If you walk past St Chads Church on Wilne Road, **Draycott** and hear organ music, don't automatically think a service is being conducted or the organist is practising. It isn't necessarily the case. Many people have heard hauntingly sad music coming from inside the locked church, and a young man named Martin Astle is said to be responsible. Martin had just been rejected by his sweetheart, and, broken-hearted, he went to the church where he sat playing the organ. After a time he left, walked down Wilne Lane to the old mill and hanged himself from a beam.

Apparently Martin is still re-enacting the incident. A courting couple were parked in the lane one evening when walking towards them from the church came a young man dressed in Victorian clothes. His attire was strange enough but they watched in horror as he passed through the wing of the car and continued down the lane towards the mill.

Three girls saw a large black coach pulled by black horses with black plumes on their heads at St Mary's Church, **Duffield**. One of the parents got in touch with the local vicar to see if an old-fashioned style funeral had taken place that day, but were assured it hadn't. They even made enquiries to see if any period film was being shot there that day but again found the answer to be no, so had the girls experienced some kind of time slip and viewed a funeral that had taken place at some other time in history?

Three Girls at Duffield saw a phantom period funeral

Clay Cross parish church was consecrated by the Bishop of Lichfield on January 25th 1851 and dedicated to St Bartholomew, but after only 27 years the churchyard was closed. The reason was said to be because its size was incapable of coping with the appallingly high death rate, although there is a rather more bizarre explanation.

A number of years ago, a member of the church whose name has never been disclosed was walking through the graveyard when he discovered that a mysterious hole had appeared in the middle of the path. He described it as irregular in shape and about a yard in width, but as he stared into it the hole seemed to grow much larger. The Clay Cross railway tunnel runs underneath the south-east corner of the churchyard and, fearing subsidence, he hurried off to get help. When he returned five minutes later there was no sign of the hole. The path and the grass verge were exactly as before with no sign of disturbance. The people he had taken to view the hole were phlegmatic and soon dispersed, leaving a very mystified man. Had he mistaken the location, was it an optical illusion or had he been hallucinating? Retrocognition is a term used to express the means of being able to look back into the past and – just as likely – out into the future. Dream prophecy is similar but more common, so had the man seen a vision of what would happen if the churchyard continued to be used?

In the neighbouring parish of **North Wingfield**, the churchyard is said to be the haunt of a mad monk. Draped in traditional brown robes, the monk has been seen wandering around, drifting between the rows of graves clutching a large wooden cross. He reputedly appears at exactly 2.30 a.m., looming out from the front of the church, but it seems he resents the intrusion of mortals. Early one morning, three members of the Paranormal Research Bureau were positioned at strategic observation points near the church when they all felt a sudden inexplicable compulsion to get away. They felt as if a disturbing presence was clinging to them, then, without warning, one of them began to recite Latin. His eyes became distant and still, his face grew pale and drawn, his body trembled with cold and fear, and his voice was almost unrecognisable. He was not a scholar and had never read or spoken Latin so this was all totally alien. He was clearly overcome by a strong physical force and it was ten minutes or more before he returned to normal.

He later told his colleagues that he had felt a tremendous pressure around him, which he was unable to fight, and had no recollection of what he had said or the meaning of the words.

A 13th-century stone sarcophagus was unearthed in **Ashover**'s churchyard many years ago. Supposedly if you walk round it three times, then lie in it with your eyes closed, you will hear the ghostly sounds of rattling chains, although why anyone should want to do this is rather baffling.

The Church of All Saints at Heath was built in 1853 to replace the 12th-century church which stood in the neighbouring hamlet of **Lund.** The two hamlets combined, but the building of the M1 and exit 29 segregated them, so the isolated old churchyard was out on a limb. The old churchyard has always had the reputation of being haunted by a beautiful woman who walks along the walls and, when walking past here was the only way for Heath miners to reach the pit at Ramcroft, they would always walk in groups, never singly, for fear of encountering her.

A gardener employed at South Wingfield Manor was driving along in his van and had just passed **South Wingfield** churchyard when all the windows suddenly and inexplicably steamed up – on the outside. This is such a weird and totally alien phenomenon that it's hard to look for a rational explanation unless we accept that a spirit had entered the van, causing the temperature inside to become colder than that on the outside.

The old churchyard at Lund where a ghostly woman in white walks around the walls

St Margaret's Chapel, **Alderwasley** dates from the 16th century but the south wall is adorned with carved heads which may have come from an earlier building on the site. The chapel is now used as St Margaret's Village Hall, but the phantom sounds of shuffling feet, an organ playing, bells ringing and singing come from an earlier time.

The churchyard of St Wilfred's at **Barrow upon Trent** is haunted by the ghost of George Turner, the famous 19th-century watercolourist, who once lived at an old farmhouse called The Walnuts. But George is no midnight artist. Rather artistically, he is seen on warm summer evenings with brush and easel seated as if painting a scene which incorporates the church.

The picturesque ruin of the old church of Thomas à Becket at **Ticknall** still stands and at the gothic window with its stone tracery has been seen the kneeling figure of a lady in blue, deep in prayer. There is also a wailing golden-haired child dressed in the clothes of the Elizabethan era, who vanishes when approached.

St Wystan's church at **Repton** is the haunt of many ghosts. The 14th-century tower and recessed spire harbours the mischievous spirit of a goblin, who appears when there is a full moon. If caught he will grant mortals one wish, provided it is made there and then and it doesn't benefit the person. The Saxon crypt is believed to have held the body of St Wystan. It is also the haunt of a hooded monk, a humming ghost and a more demonic figure bathed in wreaths of smoke, also seen sitting on a gravestone in the churchyard. A 17th-century gravedigger is also reported to

Has the Ghost of Wingerworth Graveyard been captured in this photograph?

haunt the area around the church. At one time he would stand in the trees at the edge of the graveyard and watch the village gravedigger as he worked. Pupils from the school that overlooks part of the graveyard regularly tell of seeing ghosts that wander between the graves then mysteriously disappear. Spooky tales are told in dramatic whispers in darkened dormitories after lights out.

Gwen and David White and their collie Sammy were walking through **Wingerworth** graveyard one evening when suddenly a figure welled up in front of them before disappearing into a yew tree. Sammy, who had been charging around, stopped stock still with his ears pricked up, staring at the spot.

'Did you see that?' asked David in disbelief.

'I did,' replied Gwen, and she was able to describe the phantom as a man wearing trousers and a white shirt with sleeves rolled up to his elbows, although unnervingly he was semi-transparent.

Holy Trinity Church Brackenfield on the western boundary of Ashover parish, high on the slopes of Highordish lie the ruins of the medieval Holy Trinity Chapel, a religious order founded in 1198. It's believed that this medieval ruin is a rebuild of an even earlier building which may have dated from then. Over the years, as more conveniently positioned places of worship began to emerge for this scattered congregation, the attendance at this little chapel grew less and less and in bad weather, this out of the way chapel was often empty. In 1856 it was decided to replace the chapel with the current Holy Trinity Church at Brackenfield just a short walk from the southern tip of Ogston Reservoir, on land given by Mr Turbutt of Ogston Hall, and the old chapel fell into ruin.

I featured the old chapel in my book *Discover The Amber Valley - ten walks that reveal the history of Ogston Reservoir and the Surrounding Area*. As the title confirms, it's a walk book so I was delighted to meet Wendy Butt who has a copy of my book and a story to tell. Wendy and her husband Colin had friends from out of the county staying, and took them on the walk featuring Holy Trinity Chapel. At the site they took a few photographs and were amazed to see that they had captured some amazing orbs. Holy Trinity Chapel is certainly an atmospheric place and now, if orbs are the first manifestation of ghosts, we have proof that it's haunted.

THE GHOSTS THAT FREQUENT DERBY'S PUBS

The Jacobites, whose rebellion ended in Derby in December 1745, have left a ghostly legacy in and around the city. Despite wanting to continue his march to London, the Young Pretender, aka Bonnie Prince Charlie aka Charles Edward Stuart, had to accept defeat as the decision was made to abandon their attempt to re-establish the Stuart succession, and end Charlie's dream of taking the English crown from George II. But the Jacobites' short stay in the city is reflected in paranormal activity in many of the city centre pubs. The ghost of a Jacobite/Cavalier who

The Magnificent bronze statue of Bonnie Prince Charlie in Derby

may have been billeted here in 1745 is said to haunt the **Silk Mill** public house. Lisa Roper, who owned the pub, told me how she had flipped when told of her spirit visitor. 'There's no way I would stay there alone after that,' she admitted.

The Bell has a plethora of ghosts. There's a grey lady who walks around the building, a poltergeist that throws things around behind the bar, and the most famous is the ghost in room 29, reputedly a serving wench who was murdered by Bonnie Prince Charlie's soldiers in 1745 although there is nothing to substantiate the story.

In the 1920s room 29 was the bedroom of the landlord's son, who was an asthmatic. In the middle of the night, his parents woke to hear him coughing and retching, and hurried through to his room. He was standing in the dark by his bed, bent forward, and a young girl wearing an 18th-century costume, complete with starched apron and mob cap, was standing over him patting his back to try to relieve his anguish. As the parents entered, the girl disappeared.

In the 1950s, room 29 was used as a nursery and the landlady at the time was changing her baby's nappy. She turned away for an instant and, as she turned back to the baby, realised that she had been replaced by a serving wench who was about to pick up the baby. The mother screamed and lunged forward to grab the baby, lifting it through the apparition. Although she could still see it, she felt neither a drop in temperature nor a rush of air.

In 1971, Ann Jones was working as a secretary at the Bell Inn. It was 3 p.m. and the inn was closed, but two police officers, who had just had lunch, the chef, the manager, Nick Fay plus several

The passage beside The Bell where the ghost walked

members of staff had gathered in the lounge for a drink and a chat. The chef's boxer dog had also been brought in and Ann suddenly saw the dog's hair stand on end.

'His fur looked just like a hedgehog,' Ann recalled. She suddenly felt a tremendous chill and, as everyone stared in disbelief, a grey figure appeared. It seemed to come through a closed door from the cobbled alleyway, crossed the lounge then passed through the locked door that led to the mews and outbuildings. All those present saw the figure and Dolly Millwards, the barmaid, white with shock, gave everyone a much-needed whisky.

A skull named George (despite being female) is now on display in **Jorrocks** bar. If you touch it, depending upon who you believe you can have either good or bad luck. One barman who had a stainless steel bucket thrown at him can verify that there's poltergeist activity in the basement where the skull was found. A gentleman in a blue coat with sharp features and very long hair has been seen walking up and down the stairs, sitting in the bar area and lurking on the landing at the top of the stairs. Items are moved and he gets the blame. Both the kitchen and bar staff complain that their things get messed about and moved yet nothing is ever broken and it's usually put back.

One of Derby's oldest pubs, **Ye Olde Dolphin Inn** dates back to 1520, although parts were rebuilt in the 18th century, including the section used by a local physician who not only carried out exploratory operations here but also participated in the illegal practice of body snatching. The cellars were used as a temporary morgue for this purpose and staff at the Dolphin believe that some residual energy from that time has stayed

Ye Olde Dolphin is one of the oldest pubs in Derby

there. Staff often refuse to go down into the cellars and certainly do not go there alone. Whether there is any connection between this and the poltergeist that turns the taps of the beer kegs off is unsure. But there isn't just activity in the cellars. A woman in blue is said to walk through the old lath and plaster walls. She has been seen by many customers in the pub and in the upstairs tea rooms.

The Seven Stars was built in 1680 on the site of St Helen's Augustinian monastery. Originally it was called The Plough – the astrological sign rather than a farming implement. Although its name has changed, the inn sign has not and still shows the seven stars in the shape of a plough. Seven Stars was a religious symbol and also the sign of the Worshipful Company of Innkeepers. It has always been known as a haunted pub, with footsteps and figures being seen in the bedrooms and attics, and in recent times electric lights and beer taps going off and on inexplicably. The present tenants have given the ghost the name George. Could the hauntings have anything to do with the ancient well discovered in the early 1960s, which can be seen through a glass panel in the floor of the bar today?

Opposite the Riverside Gardens on the Morledge, there's a town centre pub with the rather unusual name of **Noah's Ark**. Noah Bullock lived here but did a bit of moonlighting, making counterfeit coins in a boat moored opposite on the river. The ghost of Noah is said to haunt the building and if you should see him it's regarded as a lucky omen as it means money will soon be coming your way. But don't spend it in advance because some people say the opposite: if you see Noah, you will soon be parted from your money.

One evening the under manager of the **Friary Hotel** was drinking with customers at the bar when he saw a headless figure dressed in a black robe disappear through the panelling of the room. Several minutes later, he felt himself being pushed roughly against the bar. Could this be the same black-robed friar a former waiter claimed he once met in one of the basement corridors before the apparition vanished through a wall? Originally a friary, the modified building later became a private house owned by Henry Mosley, a Victorian printer from the Wardwick, until he shot himself in 1857. Now it is his ghost that's seen more regularly. Guests report seeing a man in

Victorian dress walking through the bedroom walls, and although some describe him as wearing a top hat, others say he holds his top hat in one hand and taps the ground with a stick held in the other. All agree he has such a dejected appearance that his sadness seems to permeate the area around him and affect any person who sees him.

THE HAUNTED HOUSES OF SOUTH DERBYSHIRE

The faded splendour of **Calke Abbey** provides a unique insight into a fine Baroque house which, like many country houses, stands on the site, and incorporates some of the fabric, of a medieval religious house of the Augustinian canons. Secularised in the reign of Henry VIII, any traces of earlier masonry have been disguised by rebuilding in 1701 and 1841, and apart from minor repairs and improvements in 1865, the introduction of the telephone in 1928 and electricity in 1962, this is the house where time has stood still.

When the house passed to the National Trust in 1985 it was in need of extensive repairs, but Calke Abbey was also ready to reveal its many treasures and secrets. Excavating for drains and electricity cables on the east side of the house exposed not only the remains of the priory buildings, but five adult male skeletons dating from the 12th to 14th centuries. Laid in a strict east–west axis suggests they were the remains of the monastic occupants of Calke Priory, and although they are now buried in consecrated ground their ghosts have remained at Calke Abbey. Various members of staff and public have seen a hooded monk in the stable block. In the old brew house, a steward heard footsteps racing along the servants' passage and galloping up the stone stairs. The family who emerged were all in shock. They had been walking along the servants' passage following an elderly man dressed in what they thought was a long, flowing coat, when he simply vanished before their eyes.

The 18th-century ticket and information office was originally the chop house where animal feed was prepared. Staff here have experienced being pinched and slapped, and on several occasions the wooden chairs used by visitors have been found next morning on the tables.

Calke Abbey, the house that time forgot, is alive with ghostly activity
Produced with the kind permission of the National Trust

In the house itself, a steward saw a figure glide through the ground-floor lobby, but the most spiritually active area is the first floor of the east wing, which until about 1860 was one of the principal apartments of the house. Staff working in the rooms below have heard footsteps walk through these rooms, despite the fact no one was there. While closing the shutters in this wing, the Property Manager Stuart Alcock has felt a strange pressure build up, followed by the pressure of a hand on his shoulder. Two spirit entities – believed to be Nanny Pearce and Lady Caroline – have both shown themselves vividly. Visitors have reported seeing the elderly Nanny Pearce sitting watching them and have taken the lady in period dress seen in the boudoir to be an actor until they enquire and find no actors are circulating that day.

I was completely unaware that, in 2004, I had captured a ghostly image on camera at **Elvaston Castle** on the outskirts of Derby. The photograph shows the different brickwork from the time when the Castle was remodelled in 1817. At one of these windows, in the 17th–century section, the ghostly figure of a lady in white is seen moving from side to side as if sitting in a rocking chair.

I took the digital photograph on an automatic setting on a bright sunny afternoon and the image looked perfectly normal until I noticed the white lines. The surface was unblemished and, after examining it in all lights and under a magnifying glass, it suddenly struck me that the white lines, almost undetectable in the sunny photograph, were exactly where and

Elvaston Castle
Reproduced with the kind permision of Derbyshire County Council

what one would expect if I'd caught the ghost of a white lady walking towards me on that path.

Could this be the ghost of Maria Foote, a celebrated Regency actress who had married the 4th Earl of Harrington, and the ghostly white lady that sits in a rocking chair at that window and glides between the castle and the churchyard? Unbeknown to me as I took the photograph, I think I was standing right in the middle of her flight path.

Elvaston Castle, on the right showing the earlier section where a ghost is seen at a
mullioned window – but have I captured a ghost on the path?
Reproduced with the kind permision of Derbyshire County Council

Accompanied by a large, white, spectral dog, this trim ghostly figure dressed in white is often seen wandering in the grounds of the castle and to St Bartholomew's churchyard in the grounds. She's perhaps looking for company because here the ghost of the Earl of Harrington haunts what is now known as the Happy Huntsman's Tree beside his grave. On his death in November 1928, the Earl left instructions that his hounds were to hunt on the first suitable day after he was buried. His huntsmen obeyed his wishes and on the day after his funeral, the hounds set off in full cry across Elvaston Park and into the churchyard where, to the amazement of the small field of followers, they were found to have stopped and were circling Lord Harrington's grave. Despite numerous attempts, the other huntsmen could not get the hounds to leave and the hunt had to be called off.

When the 5th baronet, Sir Nathaniel Curzon, later Lord Scarsdale, inherited the **Kedleston Hall** estate in 1758 he started immediate plans to build himself a new, palatial mansion. He tore down all evidence of the earlier house, diverted the road to the edge of the park, demolished all the old cottages and rebuilt the hamlet of Kedleston on a new site to the west. Robert Adam was invited to shape and landscape the 820-acre park and design garden buildings but it wasn't long before he was also put in charge of the house. The result is considered by many to be among the finest of Adam's work, a masterpiece of mid-18th-century neoclassical architecture.

Today the house and extensive parkland, which were taken over by the National Trust in 1987, are open for all to enjoy, but beware – they are haunted. A woman dressed in a blue crinoline dress and a beautiful lace hat has been seen standing perfectly still by the lake before disappearing. Visitors at first think she's in a period drama being filmed at Kedleston, until they are assured that no filming is taking place. One of the resident staff at the hall said that on moonlit evenings and foggy days, from an upstairs window she has on several occasions watched a pale, ghostly and unhappy-looking figure walk in the gardens.

Staff say the hall is almost devoid of spirits – almost! There has been the odd occasion when footsteps have been heard in the upper region of the house, doors have closed by themselves and staff have reported feeling the hairs on the back of their necks bristling with apprehension. People have reported being spoken to by an unseen presence, and in the saloon the custodian heard the sound of heavy breathing when no one but he was in there. The east wing where the family still live is said to be haunted by a poltergeist, resulting in things being moved, thrown and temporarily lost. Archivist Jill Banks confirmed that there are certain inexplicable incidents that could be blamed on paranormal activity, but assured me that whatever spirits may reside at Kedleston are all benign.

Melbourne Hall has a long history but the house that we see today is credited to Sir Thomas Coke, who altered the hall around 1696. He died without producing a son, so his daughter Charlotte inherited with her husband Matthew Lamb. Their son, Sir Peniston Lamb was created the first Viscount

Caroline Lamb haunts Melbourne Hall and its grounds

Melbourne, a title that passed to his second son William, Queen Victoria's first Prime Minister. When Queen Victoria gave her name to the Australian state, she named the capital after her Prime Minister, Lord William Melbourne, who had taken his title from this Derbyshire village.

William fell in love with the beautiful Lady Caroline Ponsonby, the young, lively daughter of the Earl of Bessborough and granddaughter of John, the 1st Earl Spencer. When they married on June 3rd 1805 she was just 16, and when not living at Melbourne in Derbyshire the family lived at Melbourne House in Whitehall, London and played host to many fashionable and lively gatherings. Less than five years into their marriage Caroline was having affairs and fell helplessly in love with the celebrated poet and womaniser George Gordon, the 6th Lord Byron, owner of the nearby Newstead Abbey. Soon Caroline and Byron became lovers; but just as soon Byron was ready to move on. Caroline pursued him with a mad, passionate obsession which didn't just cause heartache; she became mentally and physically ill.

At the age of 42, her death was hastened by drink and drugs and now her willowy figure, wearing long, flowing robes, haunts Melbourne Hall and grounds, and disappears into the intricate ironwork arbour that resembles an ornate birdcage. Does she wait there for a secret assignation with one of her lovers – the ghost in a gilded cage?

Repton is the most historic and picturesque spot in south Derbyshire, and **Repton Hall** is now part of the village's

Repton Hall, now a famous school, has a resident ghost

famous school. It was built in 1681 on the foundations of and incorporating part of the fabric of the Priory that stood on the site which, like all such buildings suffered, in the 1538 dissolution of the monasteries. The ubiquitous monk is seen on occasions, but we also have a schoolboy ghost.

Apparently in 1853, Frederick Wickham Railton, aged 14 years 8 months, in a form of initiation ceremony was forced to run up and down the gallery while the boys lashed out at him with wet towels and pillowcases. But one boy had tied an inkbottle into the corner of his pillowcase, and when the bottle hit Frederick violently on the head he collapsed and died instantly. From that day on, the ghost of Frederick Wickham Railton is said to haunt the school and his ghost is heard running up and down the gallery late at night, re-enacting that fateful event.

Codnor Castle has not been occupied since the 18th century – unless you acknowledge its ghosts. Figures flit through the ruins, the most seen being that of a Cromwellian soldier, dishevelled, unshaven and worn out.

Mackworth Castle is a mystery. It is thought to have been of 15th-century date but now all mention or evidence of such a building has gone. All that remains is the crenellated gatehouse, which has three square-headed windows to the road and a fireplace and chimney on the first floor, but the back is missing or unfinished. On certain days, a strange mist has been seen moving through the gates, and the sound of a horse has been heard on the lane near the gatehouse. Two ghosts haunt the site around the gatehouse: a man dressed in green and an old woman who smiles then fades away.

Derby has some very fine architecture. Opposite the library is the **Jacobean House** (now a restaurant and bar called The Haus). As its name would imply, this magnificent building was constructed around 1676, when the Jacobites were on the throne of England. Part of the building, which originally had five gables, was demolished in the Victorian era to make an exit through to Becket Street. Apart from that, the existing building would be recognisable to the Victorians, particularly as a phantom horse and carriage is regularly seen waiting in the Wardwick outside the house. This has been linked to the coach owned by Mrs Gisborne, the wife of Derby's mayor, but there is no record of why a headless coachman should be seen driving through the archway on the left of the building, or who the dark, mysterious figure seen standing in the entrance can be.

A Phantom Horse and carriage pulls up outside The Jacobean House

And the phantoms are not just outside the Jacobean House. Mrs Hall, who formerly worked at the house, told how she was in the upstairs rooms when she felt someone brush past. She turned immediately to see a lady in a blue dress walking out of the door and down the stairs. Mrs Hall followed but the lady had disappeared. She asked colleagues if they had seen anyone but no one had. Several days later, she saw her again walking up the stairs, but this time over her blue dress she wore a white shawl. Again the lady vanished, but on this occasion others had also seen her. Once word of this got out, other people working in the house admitted to seeing her too, always in the area of the stairs. They all agreed she looked gentle and kind, and was not threatening in any way. In fact she became so much part of the house that when things went missing, as they often did, the 'blue lady' usually took the blame. But not everyone liked sharing their space with a ghost. A solicitor who had offices in the building moved premises because he could no longer stand working in the building late at night because of the strange things that happened there when he was alone – or at least he thought he was!

St Helen's House, built in 1767, is possibly the finest surviving Georgian town house in Derby. It originally stood in 80 acres of parkland, but now it is on the A6 and its junction with the A601 is almost in the centre of Derby. After being the seat of the Strutt family in the 19th century, from 1863 to 1966 it housed Derby School, then became an adult education centre. At the time of writing this once magnificent building is about to undergo a total revamp, but before the house was erected the site was occupied by a monastic establishment dedicated to St

St Helen's House has a whispering ghost

Helen. This would account for why, on numerous occasions, a ghostly monk has been seen. Certain parts of the building have distinct cold spots, and a student in 1992 witnessed a grey, smoky figure, seemingly of human shape, descending the stairs and walking through a wall. People hear their names whispered in an eerie and chilling voice, which is rather unnerving when they believe they are alone.

The **Shire Hall**, once the social hub of Georgian society, later housed the magistrates' court and St Mary's Gate Police Station, which was locked every evening at eleven o'clock. On one particular evening the policeman had just turned off all the lights and locked the building when suddenly the lights came on again. Thinking someone was still in the building, he unlocked the door and shouted, 'Come on then. I want to go home.' There was no reply. He called again: 'I'm going home now!' There was still no reply so he walked down the corridor, and as he did so he realised that the sound of footsteps was accompanying him. He froze and the hairs on the back of his head were standing on end as he realised he now had to turn round and walk back. How he managed to do it he doesn't know but when he reached the door he flicked off the lights and slammed the door closed behind him. Two seconds later they came on again, but he left them and ran home. Next day he told his colleagues and the inspector said, 'I'm surprised at you. I thought everyone knew this building is haunted.'

Pickford House was built in 1770 by architect Joseph Pickford as his own home. It's now a museum and is said to be haunted by a young girl who dances around, oblivious to her viewers. There's also a gaunt lady who is believed to haunt the kitchen, move objects around and sometimes shout in anger at staff who are no longer there. Outside, people have reported the vision of a bent-over gentleman who appears to be tending the garden.

The Miller-Mundy family were Lords of **Shipley Manor** from 1729, but they sold out in 1944 after the area's coal mining had caused subsidence and weakened Shipley Hall's foundations. The Hall was subsequently demolished but in the area around the ruins of Shipley Hall people have sensed spirit activity, caused, many believe, by the late squire Edward Miller-Mundy. When he died, his body was buried in the grounds of Shipley Park as he had wished, but his widow had it exhumed and reburied in a cemetery in north London. Although his body is elsewhere, many believe that his spirit still roams his beloved ancestral home.

Early one September morning in 1991, a milkman named John Pratt was delivering milk to Shipley Park. As he was about to enter the gates, he saw a strange mist hovering and experienced an intense cold. His border collie, Brumas, who would normally run alongside the van while John made the rounds, had on this occasion refused to leave the vehicle, and as they drove into the mist Brumas was thrown back into the seat with great force.

John experienced this strange mist a second time when, with his wife Joy and two friends, Tony and Kathleen, he was taking a stroll on a pleasant summer evening. Their curiosity was aroused when all four of them noticed a strange haze hovering nearby. It was definitely not a mist or fog, and, as it was an old mining area, the most obvious explanation they could offer was gases escaping from closed-off, underground mine workings. Having satisfied themselves that was the reason, they began to feel rather freaked and change their minds as they moved off and the 'mist' kept up with them.

Sudbury Hall is largely the creation of one man, George Vernon, who inherited it in 1660 and almost immediately began

Queen Adelaide haunts Sudbury Hall

to rebuild the old manor house of his ancestors. This unusual Jacobean red-brick building, with patterned diapering in dark brick, has the most sumptuous interiors, with carvings by Grinling Gibbons, plasterwork by Bradbury and Pettifer, and painted ceilings by Louis Laguerre, and it is not surprising that it was used in the 1994 filming of the BBC's adaptation of Jane Austen's *Pride and Prejudice*.

It was also home to Queen Adelaide after the death of her husband, William IV. They had no legitimate heir to the throne, so his brother's daughter Victoria inherited, and the Queen Dowager chose to be independent. After a spell in the Mediterranean, she moved to Derbyshire where, in 1840, she rented Sudbury Hall from Lord Vernon, who at the time was living in Italy. Despite her love for Sudbury, her health was never good and she returned to London, where she died on December 2nd 1849.

However, it is believed that this quiet, compassionate queen still haunts the Great Staircase at Sudbury Hall, one of the finest of its kind in any English house. She is said to be dressed in black and looking ashen as she walks regally down the staircase, hesitates at the bottom step, then vanishes.

A lady dressed in an old-fashioned green velvet dress also haunts the house and is regularly seen walking along the passage towards the dining room. The ghost of the Green Lady often materialises in a green mist. My daughter Dena and I were

The impressive front entrance of Sudbury Hall

walking along the passage towards the little dining room when Dena suddenly stood stock still. By the shocked expression on her face I knew something was not right. When she'd recovered enough to speak she said she'd been confronted by a green mist that passed straight through her. I'd been no more than an arm's length away yet had seen nothing.

BIBLIOGRAPHY

Bell, David, *Derbyshire Ghosts and Legends*. Newbury: Countryside Books, 1993

Daniel, Clarence, *Haunted Derbyshire*. Clapham: Dalesman, 1975

Felix, Richard, *The Ghost Tour of Great Britain*. Derbyshire: Breedon Books, 2005

Harper, John, *Ghost Chronicles: Stories of the Paranormal*. Newton Abbot: David & Charles, 2010

Pearson, Ray, *Ghosts in and around Chesterfield*. Baythorpe: Ray Pearson, 1980

Other **GHOST STORIES** for you to enjoy from
BRADWELL BOOKS

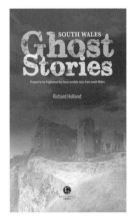

Other **GHOST STORIES** for you to enjoy from
BRADWELL BOOKS

Black Country & Birmingham
Ghost Stories

Cambridgeshire
Ghost Stories

Cumbrian
Ghost Stories

Leicestershire
Ghost Stories

Oxfordshire
Ghost Stories

Scottish
Ghost Stories

BRADWELL
BOOKS